Daddy's Apple Tree

A Collection of Poetry

Dale P. Rhodes, Sr.

Jan-Carol
Publishing, Inc
"every story needs a book"

Daddy's Apple Tree
Dale P. Rhodes, Sr.

Republished September 2017
Express Editions
Imprint of Jan-Carol Publishing, Inc
Copyright © 2001 Dale P. Rhodes, Sr.
Edited by Dale P. Rhodes, Sr. and Thomas Woolfolk, Jr.

ISBN: 978-1-945619-42-7
Library of Congress Control Number: 2017956030

You may contact the publisher:
Jan-Carol Publishing, Inc.
PO Box 701
Johnson City, TN 37605
publisher@jancarolpublishing.com
jancarolpublishing.com

Dedication

On July 18, 1994, my father underwent a total left knee replacement. He thought this would be the answer to a lot of pain and suffering, and hoped to have his right knee replaced at a later time. His plan was to improve his mobility so that he could get back to doing what he loved best, repairing lawn mowers. Plans don't always work out. In June of 1996 he was diagnosed with Dementia, a disease with the same basic symptoms as Alzheimer's. It is a debilitating and demoralizing disease that takes from you your most precious aspect of life, your memories.

Watching a person go through this is just the opposite of watching a baby taking important strides in life. Parents try so hard to be there to see their child's first steps, to hear their child's first words. With Dementia, you don't know when your loved one will lose another part of their life. You don't know when your loved one will loose memory of even you. It is difficult to watch them struggle trying to do things that used to be second nature. Then one day you stop in to say hello and you are now a stranger to them. I began to mourn the loss of my father long before his death. This feeling of frustration at not being able to help him with regaining what he had lost left me with thoughts and words that needed to come out, which reawakened my creative side.

I dedicate this, my first book, to the memory of the life and creative spirit of my father, John Lloyd Rhodes, Sr. December 25,1920-January 13,1999.

Author's Note

First and foremost, I would like to thank you for taking time out of your day to purchase and read my book. *Daddy's Apple Tree* began simply as a venting of emotions concerning my father's suffering from dementia and became a nostalgic look back at my childhood and also an outpouring of feelings from the events of my day to day life at the time. Many of the poems are true events romanticized in verse, others are simply a dramatization of the emotions inside of me. I sincerely hope that they will bring laughter and tears as you put yourself in my place and hopefully they will stir your own emotions and bring priceless memories to the surface of your mind again. Nothing would make me happier than to know that you became encouraged from my writings to pen down segments of your own life for others to read. Thanks again for allowing me to share my life with you.

Sincerely,
Dale P. Rhodes, Sr.

Acknowledgments

I would like to first thank God the Father, the Lord and Savior Jesus Christ, and the Holy Spirit for the immeasurable blessings that they have given me.

I also want to thank my family and close and special friends for believing that my words are worthy to be read and for suggesting this book project.

I would like to thank Thomas Woolfolk, Jr. for his help and advice in putting this book together.

I want to thank my mother, Frances Rhodes, for helping find all my typographical errors.

Let me not forget to thank my boys, Buzzy and Andy, for reading my work before anyone else and giving me their opinions.

Merci, pour te 'aide moi Le Rouge Tete Bandit.

Gracias por su apoyo mi amor...tres.

Contents

Damn The Disease   1

I Miss You   2

Daddy's Apple Tree   4

Christmas Past   5

Memories   6

Quilting   7

Thank You   8

A Reunion Of Leaves   10

Crooked Fingers   11

He Gave Me Two   12

Dear Mr. Scott.   14

As Long As You Love Me   16

Your Wedding Day   18

Old, New, Borrowed, Blue   20

Victory   21

Look Up   22

Her Smile   23

Just For A Moment In Your Arms   24

Love Me   25

I'm Not Me Without You   26

A Rose For You   28

I Only Dream Of You   29

That I Might Find My Ladylove   30

What Can They Do Now?   32

Two Tiny Sparrows   34

Sunrise Could Never Come Too Soon   36

Emptiness   37

Not The Same Without You   38

Furnace Vent   39

Old Love   40

Gossip Pool   42
Don't Rush Me Hubble   44
Culpeper   46
The Creatures In The Yard   48
Cinnamon Fern   49
Cool September Morning   50
Tree House Windows   51
Too Much Pie   52
Grocery Store   53
In The Salsa   54
Adventure To Disaster   56
You're The One For Me   58
Hand-Me-Downs And Yard Sales   60
Silent Cries For Help   61
What If...?   62
Vacation At The Beach   63
Daytime Soaps   64
It Looks Just Like Me   66
Lazy Day   68
To You My Dear I Try To Write   70
The Hunter's Snare   71
Yet I Know Not Who She Is   72
Blackbeard   73
When He's Gone   74
The Day   77

Damn The Disease

Damn the disease
that made his mind weak,
and stole the words from his tongue
as he struggled to speak!

Damn the disease that made me
a stranger in his distant frozen eyes
and from him, robbed the pleasure,
of each morning's sunrise!

Damn the disease
that brutally stripped away
seventy years of memories,
in just a few short days!

Damn the disease
that removed the fun from his life
and replaced it with
misery and strife!

Damn the disease
that disrupted harmony...
Damn the disease that took
my Daddy from me!

I Miss You

To only say I miss you,
would leave out so much more.
It wouldn't tell about
the many things I took for granted for.

The things I wish I had right now
just like I did before.
Hearing you say "Hi Little Boy"
as I walked through your door.

The smile that you always had
when you told of days gone by.
The answers that you gave me
when I asked you how or why.

The force within your voice I heard
when I'd done something wrong.
Tears that would stream down your face
when they played your favorite song.

I know that you weren't perfect
but right you always seemed to be.
How you could do so much
would always puzzle me.

The power and control you had
over most everything you'd do,
makes me wish that I
could do things like that too.

The way you loved us Daddy
was just the way you should.
Though you never had a lot
you gave us all you could.

"Sit down and eat" you'd often say
or "Watch TV with me."
Now everyday I wish I could
but it isn't meant to be.

"Time will heal my heart" they say
though now it may be blue,
and I must try to carry on
the way you'd want me to.

I know you're in a better place
to be forever more,
but I'd love to have you here today
the way you were before.

I LOVE YOU DADDY,
D.P.R

Daddy's Apple Tree

Life gets pushed
to the back of the mind
where there it remains...
until something reminds.

Tonight as I read thoughts
penned by someone else,
a memory came back
of my long ago self.

As a child I often would sit
where no one could see,
behind leaves on the limbs
of Daddy's Apple Tree.

My own little space
in which to sink,
when I wanted to hide
or needed time to think.

A secret, private world
only 50 feet from home,
where my mind could travel
without me having far to roam

As I reminisce now
it's so easy to see,
how lucky I was
to have Daddy's Apple Tree.

Christmas Past

The ghosts of many Christmases past
fly free all season through,
reminding everyone of
all the things you used to do.

Your little dance around the room
when the radio played your Christmas song
and the way you'd curse out loud
when the tree lights would go wrong.

The boyish grin upon your face
every time you would say...
it's not only Christmas
but also your birthday.

Tears welling up in your eyes
when on the TV screen, you'd see
Santa's cane standing in the corner
in *Miracle On 34th Street's* last scene.

Slowly unwrapping your presents
almost afraid to touch
and then always complaining
that we'd spent too much.

The holidays will never be the same
as long as we're apart
but your Christmas memories
will ever warm our hearts.

Memories

As I look at all these photographs
I remember days gone by,
some of them still make me laugh
even when I want to cry.

I guess it's true, what people say.
All good things must end.
Precious moments in life are blown away,
like butterflies in the wind.

From my greatest tragedy
there is a truth I find.
Fragile as a rose's bloom
are memories locked inside the mind.

For the loved ones in my life
I cannot make time stop,
so I will savor every moment
and squeeze out every drop.

As today drifts into yesterday
and tomorrow becomes now
I'll hold on to all my memories
for as long as God allows.

Quilting

If quilting is an art form,
Momma's certainly the Van Gogh.
With thread and yarn and cloth
she paints the canvas as she sews.

Every color, like a brush stroke
blends in perfect harmony.
The skill that Grandma passed along
is there for everyone to see.

Mothers always try their best
to keep their children safe from harm,
that's hard to do now that we're all grown
but she surely keeps us warm.

Piece to piece she joins together
until her creation is complete.
Hours at a time she works
for she would rather quilt than eat.

Thank You

I remember playing on the floor
with all my little toys,
matchbox cars, wobbling weebles
Indians and cowboys.

I never had to worry
because no matter where
my games and daydreams took me
you were always there.

When the flu bug got me,
as often was the case
you never failed to come along
and give it chase.

As I grew older
you provided me with chores
which, like any other kid,
I promptly did abhor.

Of course I would have rather
gone outside to play,
but if I hadn't done them
I wouldn't know as much today.

When I became a single dad
you were there to understand
I don't know how I would have made it
if you didn't lend a hand.

With every passing day
my boys began to do
more for themselves
and required less of you.

But then it came to pass
that Daddy was struck ill
and days for him became
a struggle, all uphill.

Once again you're called upon,
this time to care for him
as his body grew ever weak
and the light in his eyes went dim.

Never was it easy on you
but there you vowed to stay
and took care of him the best you could
in every kind of way.

I want to say that all these things
and many, many more
I so do appreciate
and will always love you for.

THANK YOU MOMMA,
D.P.R.

A Reunion Of Leaves

A reunion of leaves
from a high school tree,
a cool Autumn evening
full of fond memories.

Each leaf touched differently by time
but each touched, just the same.
Now they reconnect faces
to long ago names.

Thoughts all consumed
by many seasons past.
Friendships are rekindled
remarkably fast.

The leaves' true colors are shown
in the stories they tell,
which move some to tears
while others cheer and yell.

Not every leaf is present
on this special night,
some have already taken
winter's eternal flight.

Their spirits are alive
in those still on the tree,
as they reminisce about
the days that used to be.

Crooked Fingers

Crooked fingers, swollen knuckles
hard at work each day,
evidence of life's touch
clearly on display.

Eyes far less bright
than when they were brand new,
because of course, they've
seen the world a time or two.

Hearts, that have endured
a medley of pain and joy
with each smile and tear,
have aged with grace and poise.

Experience soaked minds
with the power to compel,
ever ready with a million
captivating stories to tell.

Take the time to watch and listen
sift through every ounce,
for when a basket's full
sometimes a little will fall out.

He Gave Me Two

As a kid I often pondered
just what life would be
if I had a son,
a real live mini-me.

A tiny hand to hold to
as I cross the street,
buying the first shoes
to put on those little feet.

A hero to root for
at his little league games,
an heir to my meager fortune
and the family name.

A child is a gift from GOD
a miracle 'tis true
and I am thankful twice as much
for he gave me two.

Though at times you make me mad
by bickering and such,
you both should always know
that I love you very much.

Precious memories of the two of you
lie just beyond my mind's door
but I still have room inside
for many, many more.

So tie your shoes real tight
and get set to run.
Let's go out into the world
and have a lot of fun.

We can take our little Neon
for a scenic drive;
or head off to King's Dominion
to enjoy all of the rides.

No matter where we go,
no matter what we see,
the best part of it all
is having the two of you with me.

Dear Mr. Scott

Dear Mr. Scott,
we'd just like to say
thank you for driving
our bus every day.

You let us be kids
so the trips weren't a bore.
You often bought us a treat
when you stopped at the store.

You always drove safe
to keep us from harm,
and if we ran late
Our dad still wasn't alarmed.

It was not hard for him
to put his trust in you,
'cause you're the best
bus driver we ever knew.

You were always so cheerful
as behind the wheel you sat,
with a twinkle in your eyes
and your "Braves" baseball cap.

We can't understand
why you're no longer here
but we'll try to remember
in GOD's eyes it's clear.

Though it's hard to accept
we can say with a smile,
we're glad we had you
even for a little while.

We will always think of you when we see a school bus...
Love Buzzy and Andy Rhodes

As Long As You Love Me

I know that it has always been
you against the world
and that you're ever ready
to give anything a whirl.

Changing that's the last thing
that I'd ever do
but if you'll hear me out
I've got a deal for you.

There's nothing wrong with
having someone watch your back,
a bodyguard just
in case of an attack.

I'm prepared to do that
if you'll just agree,
you see...you'll never be alone
as long as you love me.

In case you haven't noticed
I love you with all my heart
and of everything you're doing
I wanna be a part.

I'll be there through all the good times
and all the bad ones too.
I'll be there to try and cheer you up
when you're feeling blue.

If there's somewhere you have to go
remember my decree.
You'll never be alone
as long as you love me.

As the years pass by us
many things in life will change
but this promise that I make you
will never rearrange.

If your days outnumber mine
please don't live in agony.
Remember you will never be alone
as long as you love me.

Your Wedding Day

Long ago in Eden
God showed us the way that it should be,
creating the very first couple
when He gave Adam, Eve.

Being formed from his own rib
she was his perfect bride,
always close to his heart
and ever by his side.

If we but look at their example
and how they came about,
we will find in them
a lesson without a doubt.

A man should freely give of himself
anything his wife may need
and close to him she should always be
for from her strength he feeds.

As a rope is braided,
their lives should intertwine.
His arms become the warmth she needs;
her smile is his sunshine.

Together facing every storm
and fulfilling every dream,
the love between them flowing
like a peaceful country stream.

Now as you two begin one life
only one thing do I pray,
that your hearts always beat together
as on this your wedding day.

Old, New, Borrowed, Blue

We've been seeing each other for a long time now
I can't imagine life without you in it.
Lately I've been thinking of our future,
I don't want to waste a single minute.

You'd make me so very happy
if you'd agree to be my wife
and spend every moment with me
for the rest of your life.

I know women love to plan their wedding.
I know all the traditions too.
I don't want to steal your thunder,
but I have some things for you.

Something old...
the memories we've already made.
With you as my wife
every day will be...new.
You can borrow...my heart
just pay me back with yours.
I'll do everything I can
to make sure you're never...blue.

Victory

Let not your heart be troubled, I will surely come again
but now is not the time, so be strong and wait 'til then.

Though the world around you is swiftly closing in,
I will ne'er forsake you. I'm your savior, father...friend.

Everything that you require, I will provide for you.
I can see how much you love me, and I love you too.

Remember Job who came before and the trials that he endured.
Put your faith in Me like him and always keep your heart pure.

Though the wind is howling and the night is long,
look up to me and I will give you courage to be strong.

As the battle rages on remember...I have heard your plea,
look now at what My Mighty hand does hold, it is your Victory.

Look Up

The Lord said unto Noah, look up in the sky
and my colorful bow will surely catch thine eye.

After every rainfall, I shall put it there
to remind you of your journey and ease all thy cares.

Likewise said He to Daniel, trapped in the lion's den,
look up to me and I shall make the king of beasts thy friend.

One day three Hebrew children were thrown into the fire
but looking up to Heaven, God spared even their attire.

As the soldiers stood and watched them from without,
their Lord was there with them, and they began to sing & shout.

As the wise men traveled on that silent, holy night,
God said look up and I will guide ye with a star so bright.

It will lead ye to the manger where my son does lay,
there ye may worship him while He sleeps upon the hay.

Today he speaks to us through His written word
and tells the greatest story anyone has ever heard.

Jesus is the one we all must look up to
for he died upon the cross, to save me and you.

Her Smile

To see her smile at me,
is what I long for most.
It's more valuable than all I own
and yet it has no cost.

It warms my heart more completely
than the brightest flame,
no other in the world
could ever do the same.

Sometimes when she smiles at others
it turns me green with jealousy,
I know I shouldn't be so selfish
but I'd love to keep them all for me.

When she hurts inside
and a smile is more than she can sustain,
I try my very best
to put one on her face again.

For her sweet, playful glance
lifts my spirits when I'm down
and makes me feel as though
there's no one else for miles around.

Just For A Moment In Your Arms

I don't always take the time to let it show
but these feelings inside of me, you should know,
are different from anything I've ever felt before.
There's nothin' in this world that I'd love more
than to spend the rest of my life with you,
because every day we're together is brand new.

I'd give away everything I own,
cross the desert all alone.
I'd travel through the darkest storm
just for a moment in you arms.

When I've had a bad day and the world's not treating me right,
all I really need is for you to hold me tight.
When things go just the way I dreamed
they still never quite seem
to be enough, until I share them with you.
Because your love, my strength renews.

I would gladly give up my last breath,
take on an army by myself.
If I could, I'd fly all the way to the stars
just for a moment in your arms.

Love Me

Love me for a little while
then I will let you go
and curse the days 'til I hold you again
because they move so slow.

Time is our greatest adversary
and yet our only hope,
for to survive to claim our love tomorrow
with today's life we must cope.

Our stolen moments together
are like rare and precious gems.
We must continue to search for our treasure
it's more valuable than all of them.

As we explore the world
to realize our fantasy,
promise me tonight, my love,
that one day soon you'll never leave.

I'm Not Me Without You

When love seems to be not just right
and the littlest things cause us to fight,
it's almost enough to make me cry
and wonder what good it does to try.

Then it all begins to change when
you reach out and touch my skin.

I look into your eyes
and once again I realize,
you reside deep inside my heart
and I couldn't stand for us to be apart.

More and more I see it's true
I'm just not me without you.

The simple things in life have always meant the most to me.
flowers blooming in the spring, a gentle summer breeze.

I love to see the colors the leaves turn in the fall
and looking out the window at winter's first snowfall.

The sound of rainfall on the roof at night
and sunrise after a storm is such a lovely sight.

Seeing all these alone just can't compare
to the way I feel when I watch them all with you.
More and more I see it's true
I'm just not me without you.

A Rose For You

A rose for you the one I love.
Let it my dear remind you of,
the many precious memories
that we two have made.

Until I hold you close again
let it be your heart's aid.

I Only Dream Of You

We just said good night and hung up the telephone.
Now once again I'm getting ready for bed all alone.

You told me you want to take things real slow.
Darling I think it's time that you know.

I've been thinking of you more and more these days.
I stay so shook up, my mind is all a daze.

When I'm asleep mornin' comes too soon.
'Cause when I close my eyes I only dream of you.

Lately I've been hearing from all my friends,
"You're in way to deep" and "only fools rush in."

What else can I do, you're all I ever think of?
I don't care what they say, I know that this is love.

Time flies by so fast when you're here with me.
I can't help but feel we're meant to be

I find myself daydreaming morning, night, and noon.
And when I close my eyes I only dream of you.

That I Might Find My Ladylove

I am here without the one I love.
Though she's brighter than the stars above,
her face is lost out in the world
and my heart is deep within me curled.

It's hard to go out on my own
but I'll not rest 'til she is known,
safe with me and free from harm
gently holding to my arm.

I'll search for her forevermore
for she is all that I adore.
Why she'd leave I do not know
for she is my sweet, and I am her beau?

Her absence is more than I can bear
so I go out with only one care.
As I search my heart does speak
but no sound comes, for I am weak.

My strength is her bright smile
but my sun has not shone in quite awhile,
so I must rescue my love
to open up the skies above.

If only she could hear me now
I would find a way somehow,
to all this loneliness undo
I'd start by saying "I Love You."

As I hold tight to love's mementos
more fond for her my heart does grow,
so I'll explore unto the stars above
that I might find my ladylove.

What Can They Do Now?

What can they do now?
They're so close to the end.
If only they'd look back
they might remember when
a little spark is all it took
to set them both on fire,
but years of trials and tears
have covered the desire.

One day the two of them
seemed to share the same heart;
the next they couldn't
be any further apart.

She wants it her way,
he wants it his.
Nothing good ever comes
from behavior like this.

Harsh words are spoken,
hard feelings arise
To have a breakup suggested
should come as no surprise.

They've seen this happen
many times before,
yet every time it knocks
they open the door.

It's so hard to understand
how a love once so strong,
one that was supposed
to last all lifelong,
could now be on the edge
just about to fall.

I don't want that to happen
so I decided to call,
to say that "I Love You"
and ask if you'd like to start
over again, 'cause darling
you still hold my heart.

I hope you'll accept
this offer I'm sending,
so we can prevent
our love from ending.

Two Tiny Sparrows

Two tiny, frail sparrows
headstrong against the wind...
in each other's heart
found a loving talisman.

Together flying counter to the storm
without concern for height nor length.
Time, in the air alone, was all that was required
to renew the sparrows' strength.

Ever pressing higher
the twain endured each test,
hoping soon that they would
reach their blissful nest.

Now the hurricane is calming
and the sun is shining bright,
but there is still no cozy cottage
anywhere within their sight.

Setting down on unfamiliar ground
they, like the gusty gale, grow quiet too.
Moaning sighs of desperation
for which course to take, they have not a clue.

Bewildered, they sit silently
Wondering where, what, when, and why.
Has the raging razor storm
clipped their wispy wings
or did they just forget,
how much they used to love to fly?

Sunrise Could Never Come Too Soon

When my sun won't smile at me
my weightlessness becomes gravity.

My heavy heart and weary mind
begin a search to find,
the golden rays for which I long.
Without them my night is far too long.

I see her shine across the world
and put to shame diamonds and pearls.

Sunrise could never come too soon
for me, the one and only moon.

I care not if all the stars can see
as long as it's not hidden from me.

Emptiness

How do I ease the pain inside?
It'd be easier to stop the tide
from flowing out and in.

Your goodbye pierced me like a dart
and totally destroyed my heart.
Now emptiness abides within.

The mirror on the cabinet door
reflects the shell of what I was before...
but now I'm lifeless bones and skin.

At times the hurt does seem to fall
giving way to no feelings at all,
so there really is no way to win.

Though I rise with the sun each day,
I still can't seem to find a way
to make things right again.

Not The Same Without You

My eyes are drawn to the morning sun's
bright sparkling golden hue,
but it's just not the same without you.

My favorite music fills my ears
with it's melodic residue,
but it's just not the same without you.

All through the air, is the aroma
of spring flowers' sweet perfume,
but it's just not the same without you.

I no longer care
to see my dreams come true.
They wouldn't be the same without you.

My heart cries out imploring
that you would my pain undo.
Life's just not the same without you.

Furnace Vent

My winter weather custom
started many years ago,
as I'd sit upon the furnace vents
to feel the warm air blow.

When fever made my body
feel as cold as ice,
the first one that I came to
would be monopolized.

I would drift away to sleep
to the "swooshing" sound it made
and in the morning, to warm my clothes,
I'd put them there to marinade.

But most often, I was on my knees
my head resting in my hands
as if like an ostrich,
it was stuck down in the sand.

It used to tickle Daddy so,
he invented a new word
from then on he would laugh
and call me a "Philly-loo Bird."

Old Love

I was so surprised to see you today
and even more to hear you say
how you long to feel my touch
"'Cause I still love you too."
Many times I've wished you knew
That I have missed you just as much.

Old love can be better
the second time around.
I'm so glad that
once again we found each other.

Words can not describe
the way I feel inside
and how I've always treasured you.
The curves of your sweet face
and the warmth of your embrace,
remind me of the love that we once knew.

I've always heard, if you love someone
you've got to set them free.
Now that we're back together,
I know we're meant to be.

Old love can be better
the second time around
I'm so glad that
once again we found each other.

Gossip Pool

Be careful, they are watching.
Be mindful, they can hear.
Though you cannot see them,
they are always near.
They watch you come,
they watch you go.
They question
everyone you know
in search of any insight,
into your private life,
so that they can use it
to cause you stress and strife.
They'll sneak into your world
to see just what they can find
and take from you
personal things of any kind,
to use for their own purpose
of making your life rough.
They'll be back again and again
for they cannot get enough.
They act so nonchalant
staring from the corners of their eyes.
Don't let a single thing they do
take you by surprise.

They camouflage themselves
as your dearest friends
and secretly spread rumors
hoping to do you in.
The deadliest of parasites,
your life they wish not to take,
for they delight in seeing
how much trouble they can make.
They have many others watch you
when they can't be there
and likewise befriend you
to keep you unaware.
Just like a double agent
leftover from the cold war,
they play the part so well
you don't know what's in store.
The gossip pool is always full
and you, they wish to drown,
by spreading their stories
and hearsay all around.
My best advice is know
those in whom you do confide,
for they who are nearest to you
may not be on your side.

Don't Rush Me Hubie

One hot Saturday
near summer's end,
uncle Hubert stopped by
for a visit to spend.

In me, that day,
his match he had met
when I spoke four small words
we may never forget.

I was four or five years old
and enjoying the heat,
running free through the yard
on my two bare feet.
Crew cut hair, dirty
and sweaty from sport,
round pot belly,
just above my shorts.

Daddy cried out
without even a blink
"go to the house and
get me and Hubert a drink."

So off I went
in that general direction,
though the thoughts in my head,
were in complete objection.

In my own little world,
as was often the case,
when Daddy barked out the order
to pick up my pace.

Uncle Hubert laughingly agreed,
as if being second in command,
"yeah...hurry along little boy,
before you feel your Daddy's hand."

I, not of mind
to be anyone's boobie,
confidently turned and said...
"don't rush me Hubie."

Now after speaking my peace,
I went on my way
to fetch their drinks,
without further delay.

From that point on
the stories' not clear
but my four small words
have made conversations for years.

Culpeper

Where else in the world
would you rather live,
when the little town of Culpeper
has so much to give?

Founded in 1749, and defended by
the famous and valiant Minutemen,
They would have loved the way their town has grown
if they could have envisioned it then?

With a Blue Ridge Mountain backdrop
sparkling water at Mountain Run Lake,
and lots of beautiful countryside
to help heal any ache.

Yearly celebrations
give the town a lively spark.
The Fireman's Parade, Carnival, Culpeper-Fest
and July 4th fireworks at Yowell-Meadow Park.

Our youth sports programs
allow our kids to have some fun.
It was great to see it payoff
when our Blue Devils became State Champions.

Channel 21 and our town Web Page
keep us informed in this new Millennium.
We also have a new Theater
and Town History Museum.

We can remember our proud past
as we live and work today,
knowing that in all our country
there is no better place to stay.

The Creatures In The Yard

The storm is almost over now. The world is still alive.
The creatures in the yard have once again survived.

The song, that they now sing, is full of grace and cheer,
perfectly complimented by the thunder that's still near.

As it moves along and leaves them all behind,
they come out of their nests, to see what they can find.

Things are not exactly as they were before.
Rain has quenched their thirst and their life restored.

The heat that was too much to bear, now is gone away.
A gentle evening breeze cools them as they play.

Now the party has begun, as they scurry, fly and leap.
It will go on all night long, in the morning they will sleep.

Cinnamon Fern

Bursting up from the ground
to the delight of my two eyes,
as though it were fireworks
on the Fourth of July.

An explosion of beauty
in a bright shade of green,
yet unassumingly standing
calm, quiet and serene.

Basking in the morning sun
as it sparkles in it's dew,
proclaiming to the world
another day anew.

It's leaves unfurling
as if blowing a kiss
to God in Heaven
with grateful bliss.

Giving thanks for shade
from the afternoon burn.
Is there a more exquisite plant
than the Cinnamon Fern?

Cool September Morning

Cool September morning,
gentle breeze blowing by.
The first leaves of the season
launch themselves into the sky.

Together they free fall to the ground
in a happy, playful glide,
as if they were children
racing on invisible slides.

The sun peeks through the tree tops
bashfully bringing in the day,
like a shy little boy asking
if his friend can come out and play.

I know that autumn is now ready
to capture summer's place,
for my breath is draped across the air
like silky sheer white lace.

Only faint and distant sounds
land inside my ear,
acorns rocketing to the ground
crickets singing with much cheer.

I know this quiet moment
will not forever keep
so I'll savor every drop
while the kids are still asleep.

Tree House Windows

With my tools, I finally decided
to become acquainted,
because the tree house windows
were in need of being painted.

Sweeping through the spider webs
to take a quick inventory,
while bees buzzed around my head
defending their territory.

Scraping off the flaky, brittle watercolor
that long ago fell prey
to the harsh persistence of
Nature's power to decay.

Two abandoned bird's nests
left there to be torn down.
With the prep work done it's time
to get the brush and bucket now.

Up and down the ladder
brushing in a swift, fierce run
because my face is baking
in the oven of the afternoon sun.

I had high hopes of finishing
before the kids came home from school...
now much too late for that
my body cries out for a whirlpool.

Too Much Pie

I ate too much pie
and now my belly's pokin'.
As I sit and ponder why
I wish that I were jokin'.

On the plate it looked so good
that I could not resist.
It was as if it spoke to me
saying "eat me...I insist."

Now from my gluttony
my face does wear a frown,
because of the dessert
I simply could not turn down.

So now my stomach aches
at this overdose of sweets
because my careless mouth
did overeat.

Grocery Store

Off we go, just like we've done
a million times before,
down the road to do
the weekly grocery chore.

Ah...this basket rolls so smooth
this will be a good trip, I foretell,
as I'm drawn into the produce
by the farm fresh smell.

The kids are not fighting.
I like the song on the radio.
This is going so well,
in no time, we'll be ready to go.

I'm finding everything on my list.
There's no sign of a crowd.
With the sales paper to go by,
I'll make Momma proud.

As I hand over all my coupons,
I feel like one shrewd grocery buyer,
until the checkout person says
"I'm sorry sir...but they've all expired."

In The Salsa

Late night hunger
for at least a little snack,
I look through the fridge,
second shelf...in the back.

Ah...there it is
in a squatty glass jar.
Now if only I knew
where the nacho chips are.

My empty stomach growling
as if it's been weeks,
since nourishment of any kind
has filled up my cheeks.

I throw open the cabinet door
and drop to my knees,
as I'm digging through the snacks
I keep begging please.

Let there be just one bag
or even a half will do.
When beneath the cookies and crackers
they come into view.

Now I'm almost ready
this craving to settle.
Once I pour a glass of Pepsi
I'll be in fine fettle.

Off to the couch
I turn on the TV
and as I open the jar
what is this I see?

I can't believe this has happened
my appetite is now ruined.
I take another glance,
as if to impugn.

But to no avail
and I'll tell you why,
there lying in the salsa
I found a dead fly.

Adventure to Disaster

The sun is shining as brightly
as I have ever seen.
The air around me
smells so fresh and clean.
Today a new adventure
awaits me on a distant shore,
full of promises and of wonders
that I have never lived before.
Carefully my plans were made
and did not forget a thing,
Every tool my journey would require
I was sure to bring.

BUT NOW TRAGEDY BEFALLS ME!!!
I know not what words to speak.
How is it that a 30 second disaster
can spoil the work of many weeks?
What will those who await my arrival think
when in due time I am not there?
If only I could contact them
and my catastrophe share.
Here I am all alone
without a soul in sight
and I know much time will pass
before they learn about my plight.

To them my heart goes out
as much as for myself,
for our excursion must once again
be placed upon a shelf.
All because my mind
for just a moment slipped away
and nowhere near enough attention
to my travels did I pay.

If the measure of a man
is the joy within his soul,
then right now I must confess
that I am far from being whole.
Though my breath is still within me
and life has not come to an end
I can only wonder if we will ever
have the chance at this our quest again.

You're The One For Me

He showed up at the prom all by himself.
He greeted his friends at the door.
When they started dancing, he started thinking
"what did I come here for?"
Then he spotted her as she walked in the room
with no one holding her arm.
His heart started beating out of control.
He was captured by her charms.
He walked up to her and said
"would you like to dance?"
She looked up at him with a smile
and he thought, as he reached for her hand.

You're the one for me
I can feel it deep in my heart.
It's not very hard to see,
I knew it from the start.
The thought that you don't feel the same way I do
makes me scared as I can be.
I'll tell you some day very soon,
I know you're the one for me.

13 years had passed since that night.
Many things had changed,
but the way they felt about each other
always remained the same.
He decorated the high school gym.
Sent invitations to their family and friends.
Her sister brought her in for the surprise
and he said as he looked in her eyes.

"You're the one for me.
You've been there through thick and thin.
I love you, happy anniversary
You're my lover and my best friend."
While everyone watched
he got down on one knee.
He said "Would you do me the honor once more
'cause darlin' you're the one for me."

Many years down the road
after their kids had grown
and went on to have
families of their own.
He reached for his chest
and fell to floor one night.
She called for the rescue
as he fought for his life.
She helped him over to the couch to rest.
Looking up at her he tried to speak
and with one last breath
he whispered "You'll always be the one for me."

Hand-Me-Downs And Yard Sales

Amusing...how we change over the years.
The words hand-me-downs and yard sales are enough
to make most teenagers hyperventilate.
Wearing someone else's clothes
is repulsive to them.
At a time in life when we want our own identity, even if
we're not sure what that identity is or should be,
we do not want
anything connected to the words "previously owned."

Ah yes...but then we grow up
and among our own children's needs, mortgage and car payments
and a bucket full of other bills,
Hand-me-downs and yard sales look different now.
Like a forgotten piece of leftover Halloween candy
just waiting to be eaten, early Christmas or
an extra birthday present to be opened.
We may not like everything we see,
but always find at least one
jewel hiding in the mix.

Silent Cries For Help

Old Rag Mountain is on fire.
So much smoke pours out, it is seen for miles.
Eyes and noses burn.
The sun is too weak to break through.
Tiny ashes, scattered for miles by the
winds of destruction, fall everywhere.
They are silent cries for help,
from this gentle giant that can not speak.
Usually a pillar of immeasurable strength,
now an invalid, powerless to save itself.
At night, the blaze outlines its silhouette as if
the mountain were decorated with huge Christmas lights.

It hurts to see Old Rag burning, especially when
there is nothing I can do to stop it.
I wonder if the careless hands that kindled this flame
are hurting right now?

What If...?

What if...The last thing I ever said was I hate you?
What if...Someone needed help and I turned away?
What if...I was remembered only for hurtful things I've said?
What if...I was forgotten?
What if...I died alone?

What if...I made friends?
What if...I shared?
What if...I helped?
What if...I smiled?
What if...I said I Love You?

Vacation At The Beach

A summertime ritual,
vacation at the beach.
A lifestyle of paradise
for one week within reach.

Sunrise over the ocean
an unforgettable sight to see,
starting off the days
in perfect harmony.

Relaxing on lounge chairs
on the long white strand,
with the sound of children playing
and building castles in the sand.

Watching dolphins in the distance
without a worry or a care.
The smell of suntan lotion
in the warm salty air.

Romantic barefoot strolls
beneath a million stars,
relieve the soul of all
the daily rat race scars.

The hundreds all around me
have the same thoughts in mind,
take in all there is to see
and enjoy this special time.

Daytime Soaps

The daytime soaps are tempting
with danger and love trysts,
though the acting is not always the best
they're so difficult to resist.

Will the plot to overtake
the company succeed?
Will the father withstand
the power of his children's greed?

Will he remember who to love,
when his amnesia does subside?
Was she really kidnapped
or simply gone for a joyride?

Will their deep dark secret
finally be revealed,
or has it been
sufficiently concealed?

How was it that
their loved one died?
Was it an accident,
murder, or suicide?

All these questions will be
answered in due time,
as the daily series are full
of excitement, love, deceit and crime.

Millions nervously sit and watch
as these stories unfold each day,
others set their VCRs,
if from home they'll be away.

It Looks Just Like Me

A little boy moved into his new house
on a misty, dreary day.
"I hate this place" he said
"I can't even go out and play."
"I know you miss your friends son"
softly spoke his dad,
"but you'll see them next year in school
so it's really not that bad."
Morning came early and
took him by surprise,
as his bedroom was flooded
by the golden sunrise.
Outside his window,
on the porch next door
sat a gray haired man
that he'd never seen before.
In one hand he had a knife
in the other a block of wood.
The little boy wanted to go over
but wasn't sure if he should.

His curiosity overpowering him
he walked up and said "Hello,
I just moved in next door."
The old man replied "I know."
"Whatcha doin'?" said the little one
his eyes all open wide.
The lonely old man smiled and said
"Come see what I have inside."
So cautiously he stepped in,
not knowing what he would find.
All around the house he saw
hand-carved animals of every kind.
Many days he would go back
to keep the old man company
and gaze as he created
his wooden symphonies.
With summer almost over
and school about to start,
the old man called him over
to view his latest work of art
"This is my very best friend"
the old man said with glee.
With a big smile on his face
the boy said "It looks just like me."

Lazy Day

All night as I laid sleeping
the dreams inside my head
were quickly changing all my plans
for the day ahead.

They carried me back to supper time
from the Wednesday that just passed
and reminded me of the report
of Friday's weather forecast.

The weatherman had told
of all the pretty days to come
and how the weekend would be filled
with warm temperatures and sun.

Trying not to think of that
had proved to be a test
and it finally overtook me
during last night's rest

While the kids were eating breakfast
I called in sick to work,
then as they stepped up on the bus
I started feeling like a jerk.

To recuperate from school
they'll have all summer long,
so one day just for me
doesn't really seem so wrong.

The possibilities are endless
for a day all to myself,
the grass could stand mowing
and I need to fix that shelf.

No...I think I'm better suited
for a more leisure type of day,
enjoying all of nature
as the hours drift away.

I could sit along the river bank
to hear the water rushing by
or maybe take a scenic trip
along the Skyline Drive.

It would be nice to take a walk back in the woods
and see the beauty of a waterfall,
but I think I'll just lay in my hammock
and daydream about them all.

To You My Dear I Try To Write

To you my dear I try to write
but these meager words can't possibly
reflect the longing in my heart for thee.

With all my soul I hope and pray
this note finds you in the best of care
and somehow comforts you until am there.

As I watch each sunset pass,
in my mind it seems as though
the distance separating us continually grows.

While I am away from you
the moments last a thousand years
and it takes all my strength to hold this dam of tears.

The only thing that saves me now
are my many thoughts of you and I
and the love we've shared in days gone by.

My world's been torn apart
and necessity keeps me far from you.
My only wish is that soon I'll view
the radiance of your beautiful smile,
touch your soft warm skin
and hold you in my arms again.

The Hunter's Snare

Silently they weave their way
through the frozen dormant trees.
This band of winged intruders
their hunger to appease.

The early morning sun shines brightly
in tiny peering eyes,
as they search diligently under
grass and leaves to find their prize.

Thoroughly they scour the ground
capturing all that they can find
but though their faces hold a menacing scowl
there's no destruction left behind.

Circling the foundation
perhaps too patient to be quick,
when suddenly a predator attacks
this rooster and his chicks.

The birds run for their very lives
from a foe as rapid as a hare
but sadly one of them
can not escape the hunter's snare.

Yet I Know Not Who She Is

From the moment she fell into my eyes
my adoration could not be disguised...
yet I know not who she is.

Never before have I known superstition
but now my heart trembles at this sweet apparition...
yet I know not who she is.

I ache so to be with her
even her scent, does my soul astir...
yet I know not who she is.

I know that she lives in my home town
for I've seen her many times around...
yet I know not who she is.

If only we had some reason to meet
she would see that my heart, for her, does beat...
yet I know not who she is.

I often wonder if she knows I'm alive
and by chance, for me, her heart does thrive...
yet I know not who she is.

Seize the day, soon I must
before my heart is crushed...
yet I know not who she is.

Blackbeard

This is the story of ol' Blackbeard,
who among pirates, was the most feared.

Armed to the teeth and ready to fight.
Most men were defeated by merely his sight.

A hulk of a man from his head to the floor.
He weighed over 200 pounds and stood 6 foot 4.

Guns strapped to his chest and evil in his eyes,
his appearance foretold of many men's demise.

The dark hair on his face in rough matted braids.
Much treasure he stole from the ships he did raid.

One day the Navy tried to take him by surprise
but a turncoat's information helped prove otherwise.

After many shots were fired, he finally fell dead
and from the bow of his own boat, they hung Blackbeard's head.

They threw the headless corpse overboard, for a deep sea trip
but legend says before it sank, it swam around the ship.

When He's Gone

26 teams make their choice,
26 teams pass him on.
Then it's Shula's turn to choose,
will they miss him when he's gone?

Once he got his chance,
it would not take him long
to prove to the other teams,
that their choice was wrong.

His rookie year gave us a flash
of the brilliance yet to come
and in '84 he further showed
why he's truly number one.

All of those who tried to blitz
were taken by surprise,
as this magician's quick release
worked right before their eyes.

His touchdown passes filled the air
like bombs in time of war
he threw 48 in all
Surpassing all of those who came before.

He picked apart secondaries
with power, style and grace.
You knew a score was coming soon
when you saw that look upon his face.

He completed many passes
to Rose and Moore and others
but there was something very special
between Marino and the Marks Brothers.

The names would change along the way
to Jackson, Ingram and Fryar
Greene, Smith, Paige, Clark,
Edmunds, Abdul and Byars.

Nowadays he throws to a whole new set of men
Johnson, Conrad, Greene, Gadsden,
Thomas, McDuffie and Martin.

Though the years have changed him some,
as time so often does.
He's still the same GREAT QUARTERBACK
as he ever was.

But now the football world
has sharply taken aim
and for every loss the team endures,
he shoulders all the blame.

Finding fault in how he plays
on this the press does thrive,
even when he leads the team
on a winning drive.

They've turned their back on the man
that's always played with great desire
and now they eagerly await
the day he does retire.

No longer can they see his worth,
that the field is where he belongs.
When he steps down, it's the game that will lose.
Will they miss him when he's gone? ...I WILL

The Day

With an awfully heavy heart
and eyes that sorely cried.
I sat and watched the TV screen
the day that football died
No...not the sport as a whole
but the part that was inside,
of me for oh so many years
and which I could not hide.
For he, had said goodbye that day
with his family by his side
and left behind a great career
that filled us all with pride.

Many Sunday afternoons I watched
with eyes all open wide
the offense up and down the field
with number 13 as it's guide,
as he would take another
defense to divide.
They blitzed him from the front
and also the backside.
But with great presence
up in the pocket he would slide
and throw a strike to his man
to catch in perfect stride.

Sadly on March 13, 2000
my hero did decide
that it was time for him
to take that sunset ride
and though he said "This is a happy day"
I could not help it if I cried
for I lost a part of my innocence
the day that football died.

Dan Marino
13 forever

About the Author

Dale P. Rhodes, Sr. was born in Culpeper, Va. He is the son of Frances White Rhodes of Schuyler, Va. and John L. Rhodes, Sr. of Charlottesville, Va. He is the next to youngest of eight children, having six sisters and one brother. He was raised in Lignum, Va., a suburb in Culpeper County.

He was educated through the Culpeper public school system, attending Pearl Sample and A. G. Richardson Elementary Schools, Culpeper Junior High and High Schools.

He has been employed as a laborer, cook, dish washer, quality control inspector and group leader.

He is a single father of two teenage boys, Dale Jr. (Buzzy) and Andy and considers this his greatest achievement in life.

Dale has published two other books, "If Only..." and "Next Summer." Dale has had individual pieces appear in print before. "I Miss You" and "Culpeper" both were printed in the Culpeper Star Exponent newspaper. "Her Smile" was published in the International Library of Poetry's anthology, "Chasing the Dawn." "Just For A Moment In Your Arms" was published in the Amherst Society's, "American Poetry Annual 2000." "Damn The Disease appeared on the compact disc entitled "The Sound of Poetry" recorded by the International Library of Poetry.

"Like" Dale Rhodes Books on Facebook: www.facebook.com/dalerhodesbooks.

Coming Soon

The City on a Hill series

If Only is the story of guardian angel Thaniel and his struggles to lead humans to the God he loves.

and

Next Summer is the story of best friends who turned their senior class trip into a mission trip.

"Like" Dale Rhodes Books on Facebook

www.ingramcontent.com/pod-product-compliance
Lightning Source LLC
Chambersburg PA
CBHW032050040426
42449CB00007B/1051